AF322723

WHAT I WISH I KNEW

*This book I dedicate to all of my lovely nieces and nephews,
Auntie loves you!*

Table of Contents

Thank You

Thank you for all your support, thank you for showing up in the world as yourself. In the pages to come you will be taking your first step to helping make this world a better place.

You never know what someone may need to motivate them in the right direction. So please share to help this book reach billions of people all around the world.

Sincerely: Aneesa El Amin-Sims

I wrote this book for all the young women and young men of the future. I thought my life would look much different from the reality in which I'm living. The truth is I didn't take my life seriously until having to learn many life lessons. I still have a lot to learn and like most of us I don't plan to stop learning for as long as I live. But this book isn't about me, it's more about the lessons I've learned from others as well as myself and the things you should do to avoid some costly lessons. This book was written to help you navigate to adulthood much easier than myself. Life is definitely a journey and I want this guidebook to help you realize and discover things about yourself, and the way the world works without many growing pains in the process.

I made this book in regards of your time in mind, so it's short and sweet. While this book was written for teens and parents, no one is perfect, so it doesn't matter if you're reading this book at 14 years old or 54 years old. I am sure that the contents of this book will be beneficial to your life. Teens use this as a tool to learn more about your parents to avoid some of the mistakes they made in their life. Parents use this book as a tool to bond with your teens, to understand them better and help them navigate into adulthood the way they would like. Learning from the mistakes of others is just as important as not making the same twice. Shaping the future is our responsibility for as long as we have breath in our lungs. I am certain this book will help us all in positively shaping the future.

Chapter: 1
Pressure

I'm not sure if you are familiar with the term "Rat Race". But according to Merriam webster dictionary:

- A rat race is a strenuous, wearisome and usually competitive activity or rush.

Reading that, I immediately think routine and as you know life can feel like that when you experience constant repetition. You don't live in this world alone. Everyday people are lined up, it feels like competing for the same positions. That being said, the world is in constant hunger looking for new positive innovations and creations from people like you, paving the way for the future.

The world we know is filled with many people doing just about the same thing without thinking twice about it, not even questioning why they're doing it. Bear with me for a moment, I want to give you a visual. Okay, so your born and hopefully blessed with both parents in your life that prepare you for schooling. You get to preschool and experience 14-15 consecutive years of schooling where you might have been told (Don't ask the wrong questions, keep your head down and get good grades). Well, what are the wrong questions? I'm glad you asked. Some may say that these are touchy topics:

- Questions that threaten the existing political system.

- Questions that threaten the structured education system that has had the same learning material forever.

- As well as questions that are outside the box, (meaning questions that cause the teacher to think outside of the school curriculum in order for a student to get a response).

Which brings us to the systematic gold standard: A continuation of schooling in college after 14-15 years of learning. Once you graduate high school everyone is hoping you are conditioned to thinking that college is a no brainer. What's an extra 2-8 years right. Then after all that work you put into your education; you get a beautiful 6 figure bill depending on how unlucky you are. Side bar: I want you to know that I'm not against traditional schooling. Knowing all your options before wasting away thousands of dollars and years of your life you can't get back is important for me to share. Now that you have your college degree that you paid for twice now, investing not only your time and money. You get to start at the bottom of your field to work your way up. I'm sorry in advance for the next bit of information you are going to receive but according to the Harvard business review 2/3 of college graduates struggle to launch their careers. Meaning, out of all the college graduates 1/3 of them can look forward to being securely employed in the field they studied for. A positive take away all college students get the opportunity to create is a family away from home. When they are able to mingle among other students from different backgrounds and find their flock. Getting to the rat race concept let's say you get in your field of study and are doing well for yourself. Then next thing you know your moms asking you when she's going to be a grandmother and I'm sure you now see how the cycle repeats. If you want to know more about the "Rat Race" Robert T. Kiyosaki talks more in depth about it in his 1997 book "Rich dad Poor dad".

Parent Expectations

I'm going to get this out of the way before diving into this section; (mom, dad, or stepmom, stepdad) we love you but please understand! Often times our parents mean well even if it doesn't seem like it, the pressure they put on you is sup-posed to motivate you to A. Be just like them or B. Be better than them. But often times than not it can drive a child to have stress, anxiety and focusing/ depression problems. Some parents expect the best (referring to the- all "A" gold standard) but everybody's best doesn't look the same. I'm not going to even deep dive into talking about sports or extra curriculum activities on top of having to produce top grades. Many research studies have claimed that parental pressure is one of the leading causes of increasing rates of student suicides in India. I am sure that part of the increase of suicides here in the U.S. are related to parental pressure for perfection as well. Please never let the pressure get to that point of no return for you. Reach out to a trusted adult or relative that can help you speak to your guardian if you don't feel strong enough to speak up for yourself. Your life is too precious to be wasted!

Perfection is a psychological unattainable expectation that can never be achieved by any one person. While it is known for parents to pressure their children there are times when the child puts that kind of pressure on themselves. Which can be good at times, but you should never suppress your social, physical, or mental health to attain such goals. There will always be space for improvement and getting better in anything you choose to do. The only thing I've ever known to be perfect are moments in time.

"Do today what others won't and achieve tomorrow what others can't".

-Jerry Rice

Peer Pressure

Peer pressure can look like keeping up with the Jones's as some adults may say. The phrase "Keeping Up with The Jones's more so highlights the material gratification of success one looks to achieve or desires in life based on the material success of others. All in all, both peer pressure (doing something you may not want to do) and keeping up with the Jones's by (living an unreasonable lifestyle based on friends, colleagues, or family) is bad! Here's the real in 2021 there were 473, 349 bankruptcies in the United States which means that families suffered due to mismanagement of funds and living beyond their means. I want you to know that our appearance is important and does affect the way people perceive us initially. So, it's important to show up looking your best! But it's important to stay within your means, it may be difficult but it's necessary because you never know who you may encounter. You always want to look the part, so you never miss an opportunity, but you don't want an uncomfortable life so be mindful in your choices. TIP: accessories have the ability to take any outfit up a notch. You should never be ashamed of where you come from even if it's humble beginnings. It may define how you start but it definitely doesn't define or determine your final destination in life.

I remember being in second period in 10th grade and being offered a water bottle with no label. By the grace of God, I asked what was in it and at 9:45am I was being offered vodka (WILD I KNOW). Listen, my parents never talked to my sister or I about not taking drugs, drinking alcohol or having sex. We I guess just assumed that we shouldn't do it and if I'm being honest, I was never in a rush to experience any of those adult activities. I'm not going to tell you not to partake in those activities either, but I will say that you should research the side effects before taking or doing anything you've never done. I'm not saying that you should be just like me, I'm saying that you just have to do your own research and make your own educated decision based on the facts you find. (Don't just take anyone's word for it)!

I am going to share some basic information that most of you know that is just surface level knowledge but a reminder. Drugs and alcohol alter your state of consciousness and control. Which could result in crimes being committed and the harming of innocent people. Sex can lead to STI's and STDs, or an unplanned pregnancy. I know your probably thinking that I'm being dramatic but if I'm going to be real with you, I have to be 100% through and through. I want you to win in life and to do that means knowing the pros and the cons beforehand so you can make educated decisions, it's your life! I'm just here to help you on your journey. Saying "NO" should definitely be a part of that journey, especially in the event when you don't want to do something, even when everyone else is saying "YES". Saying "NO" is a power move many people don't respect until you're an adult, but you should try it out and see how good it feels to have that kind of control in your life. You should expect respect when you conduct yourself in a respectful manner! I will spare you all the addiction, gateway, DUI and rehab talk, you have probably heard a million times now and leave you with:

*"One can have no smaller or greater mastery
than mastery of oneself".*

-Leonardo Da Vinci

The choices we make can greatly affect our lives and we have ultimate control to do, or not do certain things that shape our stories. You are responsible for your own choices and adults own their choices no matter the outcome. Leaders are always needed in the classroom, workspace and in various areas of business. The best leaders take ownership not only of their own mistakes, but at times in group settings, the ownership of mistakes done by others, or in Jocko Willink and Leif Babin book "Extreme Ownership" the fault for a failed mission. In my early twenties two adults, one in their thirties and the other one near thirty years old gave me some questionable advice. I was told that your twenties are the time in your life when you're supposed to sleep around, do drugs, drink and party, not really think about the consequences. Listen, I know what you're probably thinking, they clearly didn't care about me, right? I actually don't believe that to be true, sometimes people give advice based off their own beliefs and life experiences. People can give you crap advice even adults, that doesn't mean you should take it for face value. Everyone isn't qualified to give you advice and you have to be discerning when taking advice from people, including family. No one knows everything and sidenote I don't feel a way towards those people who poorly shared that advice with me. Before you take advice from someone ask yourself, would you mind trading places with that person? If the answer is (NO) then run that same advice past a few people, you trust and see what they have to say before going forward.

FYI Your Voice Matters

If you are reading this as a young woman or a young man, I want you to understand that what you have to say matters more than you know. You are the future politicians, U.S. house of representatives, senators, leaders, law writers, activist and you should make noise and speak up about topics you are passionate about, that speak to you and make you motivated to not only change yourself but that will help positively change the places we call home. Understand while all of our voices matter it can be difficult to get your parents undivided attention and respect when discussing things that are important to you. Your words can seem to fall on deaf ears, but never let that stop you from expressing yourself and just know that someone will want to listen, if it's not your parents then I suggest reaching out to another family member/ teacher or trusted adult. Shine bright my dear and be the change you want to see in the world!

If you are a bit more mature and you work with others or have difficulty being heard amongst your friends or family. I recommend you practice reciting affirmations to empower yourself. That may help you find your voice and help you convey whatever

you want to say with conviction. I want you to know that your feelings are valid, and your voice is strong, and needs to be heard. Your ideas are important, and your contribution accepted and invited. Silence can be golden, but there are other times when saying the right thing or the thing that needs to be said can change how people see you and be quite impactful. Be a light and help light other candles on your journey.

Chapter: 2
Who Wants to See You Win vs. Who Wants to See You Fail

In a world filled with ego's you have to be seriously careful with who you trust. I say this because a lot of people can be selfish and only think about what they want in any given situation. This has been proven in the music industry especially as it pertains to youth artist contracts. Family have been known to sign some pretty terrible deals, mismanaging money and at the worst, stealing from artist. Learn how to go over contracts so you know what your signing, I recommend the book "contract law for dummies" written by Scott J. Burnham. I also recommend you learn how to manage your money properly in your teens, so you don't run into financial issues with financial advisers, managers or parents in the future. One thing you can count on, is you having your own back and best interest at heart. You would be surprised by how many situations have occurred due to an envious or jealous relative. I'm not telling you that you can't trust anyone, I'm saying you should use caution and your best judgement. Out of everyone in the universe there is God as well as yourself who you know hands down, without a doubt, want to see you succeed and win at life. PLEASE NOTE: You should never focus on those who aren't wishing you well, those people whomever they may be, aren't even worth a thought. However, you should pray for those imbalanced, confused and lost souls because they could be going through a difficult time unbeknown to you.

"The first step towards success is taken when you refuse to be a captive of the environment in which you first find yourself."

-Mark Caine

When your young it's easy to be influenced without taking notice. So, you need to pay attention to what you listen to, what you internalize on your day to day and who you befriend.

Unconsciously you could be picking up negative traits or taking on a negative attitude. You can't control every situation, but you can control how you react to it. You can control who you spend time with and who you choose to be, in your friend circle, so choose wisely. It's nice to also engage with people who don't necessarily agree with you all the time. People who challenge your own thoughts and processes help you grow and understand different perspectives as was discussed in the book "The Secret Principals of Genius" by I. C. Robledo. People have to be around you as much as you have to be around others. Be mindful of the kind of person you are and switch it up if you don't like the person you are becoming.

Everyone doesn't want to see you win! With that comes fake love and fake support. You have to watch out for those people because they think you're going to win, and they want to be there for the success to in simplistic terms "use you". Which indeed is an ego problem as well as a lack of integrity problem.

Don't worry if you don't give anyone one cent, you'll spot them. Anyone who makes you feel like they are expecting a handout, test them indirectly to find out what you need to know. You shouldn't feel obligated to give a family member or a real friend one cent when you're on your come up.

> *"There is light in the darkness and darkness in the light".*
>
> *-Aneesa El Amin-Sims*

A bully according to webster dictionary is a blustering, mean or predatory person who, from a perceived position of relative power, intimidates, abuses, harasses or coerces people, especially those considered unlikely to defend themselves. Bullies can be found at work, at home, in religious settings, schools and even amongst friends. The first step to dealing with a bully is to be understanding, whomever is responsible for your frustration or pain is also in pain of some kind as well. That knowledge doesn't excuse their behavior, but it definitely can help you feel better knowing that their actions probably have nothing to do with you, other than the hurt they inflict. You may already know that bullies have probably been victims of bullying themselves or have experienced some sort of trauma that has never been healed. That being said there are two ways you can put an end to that kind of treatment without an outside source: 1) You can pay them no mind, ignoring them would make them realize their words are doing nothing to you but making them realize how much of jerk they are being. Remember energy goes where attention flows! 2) You could be really kind and bring gifts to the person harassing you, that person may just need a friend and the best way to find out the root cause to a bully's troubles is inside the friendzone. It's hard to continually be mean to someone being kind to you. Whichever you decide, know that hate + hate can only result in hate but hate + love can equal change. There's more than what's beneath the eye.

FYI Safety First

Have heard that the world is a dangerous place? The answer is probably yes, right? So, you have to take necessary precautions when leaving the house as follows.

1. No matter if you are female or male you must always be aware of your surroundings.

2. Ladies, please consider taking self- defense classes to even the field if you ever have to defend yourself, it's always better when they don't see it coming. (That being said you don't want to broadcast your skills either)!

3. Gentlemen protect young ladies and women if a situation presents itself when you are near, intervene or call for help. (Never be a by-standard with a phone)!

Sisters, please understand in order to change the way things have been we have to do things differently. We have to be able to defend ourselves and stop giving predators the opportunity to even think they can try it. We have to start arming our beautiful young girls with the same self- defense courses as well, being a victim will one day be a thing of the past, if we can all get on board with this new program. Young men, besides standing up and protecting young women from harms-way. Please speak amongst your peers so that we can stop the inappropriate encounters, harassment, dialogue and overall behavior towards the entire female population. We can all ensure safer environments if we do our part and work together to create that change.

Chapter:3
Assets & Liabilities

-An asset is a useful or valuable quality, person, or thing, an advantage or resource.

Example: assets are things like homes, gold and well- known art. Items that appreciate are also considered assets too like stocks, gold and Birkin bags.

-A liability is something for which one is liable, an obligation, responsibility, or debt.

Example: an easy example of a liability in simplistic terms is as follows: bills, bills and more bills.

Successful people like luxury items same as most of you but they do things differently than most of society, that's why they are called the 1%. They take the money they earn, or money borrowed and buy assets to make their money work for them. Once they double their money or triple it, they are left with options, to pay back their lender or cover their investment. Only then do they buy their luxurious good, this process is easy to repeat and that is how their money multiplies, that's one of the ways the rich get richer.

This may come as a surprise to you, but you can see similar qualities in people. They have the ability to add value in your life or they can bring you down emotionally, physically and spiritually as a liability can do.

"Try not to become a person of success, but rather try to become a person of value".

-Albert Einstein

When Albert Einstein talks about a person of value in the above quote, he's referring to a skilled individual. For example, people who know more than one language, someone who listens well, people who know how to defend themselves and others with martial art techniques or kickboxing skills etcetera, are things that people find beneficial in others. As well as just knowing how to do things others may not be knowledgeable in. The more you can do or know how to do, the more valuable you appear in the eyes of others. Ask yourself the question are you an asset or a liability? I also recommend that you learn and become fluent in at least 3 languages including your native language. By learning skills and bringing your capabilities up, you will be able to enrich the lives of people you know and meet. Be open to learn constantly so that you can also be of high value in the lives of your family, friends and significant other.

"Success is where preparation and opportunity meet.

-Bobby Unser

FYI Credit Cards

You may have heard that credit cards are the devil, a scam, free money and I'm here to tell you how you can successfully avoid thinking the above statements. Credit Cards have funds that are issued by institutions like Wells Fargo, Chase and Goldman Sachs, that allow you to borrow money for interest. Blaming credit cards for one's lack of discipline in spending by not owning the result of your actions, is a bad habit. I didn't learn about credit cards until I got my first credit card at 19 years old. You can guess what I did with my lack of knowledge in that area, I ran that card up until it maxed out. It was the worst thing I could have done, and to get my balance down to a healthy limit took a great deal of discipline and determination, all jokes aside. I definitely don't want you to repeat my mistake so here are some things you can do to have a successful and healthy credit history.

First thing you should know as a minor is that your parent or a trusted adult can help you establish credit through their own credit line.

Please note: Your credit becomes a part of your identity when you turn 18 and while most 18-year old's start out with no credit, you can have an established credit history allowing you access to more funds than the average 18-year-old. Be discerning when you pick an adult to assist you with building your credit because adults can be extremely irresponsible when managing other people's money let alone their own. This can at times result in a parent using their children's social security no. for water bills, electricity bills and other household bills. Never use more than 30% of funds available at any given time, unless you are going to make a large first payment to bring your balance down under 30% usage. You can avoid paying interest by paying your statement balance sometime during the grace period which is within 21 days after the statement closing date, but make sure to pay before the payment due date. If you can help it don't just pay the minimum due try to pay more than what is owed, it's always best to stay ahead. When you are first starting out and building your credit, only spend what you have in cash available, so you never have to struggle making payments. If you want a better understand of this section, ask a trusted adult if you can be present when they pay credit card bills so they can help you go over a statement in real time.

Wealthy people let their credit work for them by investing in art, real estate and businesses instead of leveraging their own personal capital. The better your personal credit the more access to money you'll have when establishing business credit cards. Success is for everyone! I hope this information reaches you in a way that allows you to avoid the mistake I made. If you are reading this and are a bit more mature, it's never too late to correct mistakes, you just have to buckle down and organize what you owe. Focus on paying the smaller bills and then tackle the bigger bills one at a time, keep your head up no matter where you are on the credit scale, whether building credit or fixing a credit score. You got this!

Chapter: 4
Relationships

If you are atheist this next paragraph may not be for you, but I dare you to continue reading on anyway. As you may know relationships are extremely important but the one that matters most is the one between you and God. All that we are and all that we see wouldn't be possible without creation. The chances of you being born just the way you came into this world is quite miraculous if you think about it. Praying to God just helps you through your life journey no matter the bumps in the road you face. God is everywhere and nowhere all at once, a powerful source of energy that plays a role in each and every one of our lives. So, it'll be wise no matter who you are, what you've done or what religion you practice to always thank God for that of which you have. Especially when seeking answers because God always comes through and shows us the answers we seek; even if we are unaware of what they are.

"There are two types of people who will tell you that you cannot make a difference in this world: those who are afraid to try and those who are afraid you will succeed".

-Ray Goforth

Relationships between children and parents can be complicated, like a love/ hate relationship. Parents want the best for you in most cases and sometimes they aren't even certain in how they can help their children. Bonds between parents and their children are very important and as children it's important to remember that parents don't know everything. They share with you the things they've been taught and during certain times of our life, the experiences they once lived. We have to remember this because I know when your young you think your parents know everything or are supposed to know everything. But the reality is that they are still figuring a lot out themselves and are learning same as us just at a different level in life. Being respectful to the people responsible for raising you is a must. You can't expect respect if you don't give it. We have to give our parents grace because we are all in this experience together, figuring it out as we go. So be mindful when in the presence of your parents because they love you and at the end of the day want what is best for you, even if they don't know what that looks like all the time.

When it comes to friendships, they have many highs and lows like a rollercoaster but one thing I know is that clear communication is crucial. Miscommunication and assumptions are the leading cause to break ups in friendships, marriages and just about any other relationship you can think of. If you value the other person, you should always grant them that of which you would want if you were in their shoes. Disagreements are normal and make relationships interesting because they allow you to realize and possibly appreciate the difference in the other person. Relationships between significant others and friendships are very much so similar because no matter where you end up down the line. In the beginning your just getting to know one another, while trying to find similarities that could bring you closer together, creating bonds.

Generally speaking, relationships are very important in everyday life. They help us understand each other, allowing us to share epic moments together and can help us navigate through life better. The world is filled with billions of people, and you may not know this but at one point in history all the continents were connected. Since the beginning of time, species have all relied on each other for survival and we were created in that way to need each other for survival. As a people from many different backgrounds and walks of life we have separated ourselves just as the continents. I still believe that our survival is reliant on our relationships whether it be with a neighbor, friend, family member, coworker, or significant other. We have to get back to community in order to strengthen and create strong bonds with the people in our lives. We were created to fit in the universe like a piece to a puzzle, to work together and create. To share an individual but wholistic experience that connects us all.

Understanding plays a huge role in relationships and it's like the best friend of communication, they don't always get along, but they are both needed in any healthy relationship. There are many levels to understanding but I find the silver lining to be when you can see another-persons views or opinion and respect it, not having to necessarily agree with them. We all see the world differently due to our life experiences and I think it's great to have people with different outlooks, backgrounds and opinions helping to challenge the way we not only see each other but see the world.

"To succeed in life, you need two things: ignorance and confidence".

-Mark Twain

The second most important relationship is the one you have with yourself. How can you expect someone outside of your family to love you unconditionally if you don't love yourself in that way. I'm not going to get too deep talking about self-love, but I will share the basics. Get to know yourself, the likes and the dislikes. Understand your flaws and figure out if they're things you want to change. You should also learn how to please yourself. By accomplishing this you will help prevent premature childbirth at any age. If you are a teen and you have questions on the matter, reach out to a guardian or doctor who specializes in that field. I'm sure they'll be happier explaining how to do that process vs. having to go pick out baby clothes at target before your graduation. Knowing your body is your responsibility and once you have that knowledge of self you can introduce someone else to the wealth of you. This process will help you gain a strong sense of self and give you the confidence you need to do anything your heart desires. Self-discovery is the first step to preparing yourself for a romantic partner. I wasn't prepared in that way and experienced heart break because of it. Searching for love externally instead of looking within and it all could have been avoided had I taken necessary steps to self-discovery and self- love at an early age. So please take this section seriously because I want to be responsible for many of you not having to experience such sadness due to a lack of knowledge of self.

You should also start listening more than conversing in your existing relationships. This exercise will prepare you for when disagreements or oppositions occur in any relationship you establish. You can respond better when you have fully understood the position of someone whether you agree or not, it doesn't matter until you've whole heartedly heard the other person out. I want to prepare you for success in as many areas of your life as humanly possible and I'm writing all this because I wish I had this information when I was also a youngin growing up. Make sure your cup is never too full, constantly be open to learning, evolving and growing in your life. Please remember each one, teach one. When considering a relationship remember to bring 100% of you to the table not 50% of you. A power couple is 200% so discuss where each of you are individually in every aspect of your life so you can properly enjoy one another. There is nothing wrong with someone not being 100% whole, but you have to be transparent in the beginning so nothing surprises anyone down the line. When building a strong foundation in a romantic relationship, and as stated in Eve Eschner Hogan and Steven Hogan's book "Intellectual Foreplay", you want to make sure that there's a mind connection, a spiritual connection, an emotional connection and then body connection. In that order to make sure you're not rushing into a relationship without knowing someone well enough. Take your time with these connections, in today's time people tend to connect in a couple of areas, not even considering the others, but they're all important when creating strong bonds and everlasting love.

Message to Her

Some Talk

Some Walk

Some Sing

Some Yell

Some Whisper

Some Warn

Some Squeal

Some Soothe

Some Yelp

Some Help

They're all beautiful when they're being themselves.

-Unknown

You are a miracle and all that you are is special because God made you to perfection. You may not know what you want to do or who you want to be in the next few years, and that's okay, be patient with yourself. Make sure to put yourself first because in life people will always need you, but you won't be able to show up for them how you want if you aren't whole. Love yourself unconditionally first before you expect or allow others to love you unconditionally. In life there will always be people trying to put us women against one another, never fall for that never ending scam. Your greatest competitor will look back at you in a mirror, you should always strive to outdo you. As women we are stronger united vs. separate and that is true in many aspects in life. Many people will try to feed you lies, be wise and learn from other people's mistakes and be smart by searching for truth. Another young women's brilliance, beauty, creativity, should never threaten all that you are. Never allow that to get in the way of your own genius, beauty, or creativity and cheer on the greatness in others so that when it's your time, people will be thrilled to do the same for you.

"A candle loses nothing when it lights another candle".

-Thomas Jefferson

Message for Him

My ego gets in my own way

A barrier to my learning

When I should eat some humble pie

Instead, my pride is churning

My ego tries to save me

From losing face and trials

When I should know I am enough

Worthy without qualifiers

My ego is a complex thing

The balance is the key

Humility to listen up

And believe in my own being

Your life is extremely significant and how it is lived is entirely up to you. Learn to balance your emotions, master discipline and practice humility; that will get you where you want to be in life. Learn what it means to love yourself and take care of your health before expecting someone else to love you in that way. Men die at a faster rate than women statistically, the reason is because women are better at releasing their emotions by journaling or crying or speaking out their frustrations to a trusted friend/ family member or a therapist. You may think that emotional release outside of fighting is weak, but despite your opinion, it is effective. It takes great strength to forgive, let go, and release that kind of energy. If you need to have those private moments, then take them but you have to release that energy, or it may manifest in a negative way, through an illness or a physical or verbal outburst.

"ONE CAN HAVE NO SMALLER OR GRETER MASTERY THAN MASTERY OF ONESELF"

-Leonardo Da Vinci

Where would you be if it wasn't for your mother? Women are to always be respected and treated kindly. Treat others like you would want to be treated or better. Don't do as you see in life, do as you know, be the example even if it is to someone much older than you.

Romantic Tips: Ladies are attracted to ambitious gentlemen. Be honest with yourself and offer that same transparency and kindness to others. When your pinched for cash think outside of the box, you always get an "A" for real effort. You must prioritize, there's no such thing as I didn't have time. You let women know where your head is by how you prioritize them in your daily schedule. Listen intently not to respond but to understand and once you have done that let your ego take the backseat while you reply eloquently.

Chapter: 5
What time is it?

*"You don't have to be great to start, but you
have to start to be great".*

-Zig Ziglar

Life can be loud when you live in a city and deal with

constant music, radio, podcast, tv, phone calls and work not to

mention your social life. To be successful requires you to get fo-

cused by eliminating distractions and making space for your

goals. I know you probably heard the saying "life is too short"

and the reason why older people say this is because they waited

until their 30's to take their life serious. I'm sharing this infor-

mation with you hoping that you start today setting your life up for success, so you can enjoy it in your 30's and 40's, while your still young. You'll be much better prepared than your parents and me.

We are all given the same 24 hours in a day, it's how we use that time that makes all the difference in the world. Once it has passed you can't get it back and if you don't make the most of it while it's present, you will feel like it was wasted away. I've noticed the older you get the more you value time and wish you can hold on to youth for as long as possible and if you are under the age of 18 youth typically desire to be older. Please don't choose to waste your time especially when your young, seize every moment God gives you. You can accomplish so much in your life and help inspire the generation that comes after you. Mel Robbins talks about applying immediate action from your thoughts in "5 second rule". She explains how it takes 5 seconds to talk yourself out of doing something, so she insists that you count up to 5 and immediately taking action before you change your mind. If you put in the necessary time now you will be mentally, physically and spiritually prepared for anything life throws at you.

"You don't have to see the whole staircase, just take the first step".

-Martin Luther King Jr.

Get real about the things that are serving you, people included and let go of anything and anyone standing in the way of your success. Make a list write down the positive people and productive things you do on one side of the paper and on the other side write down the negative people and bad habits. This exercise will give you a clear visual of the work you have to do, and I will provide an example for you. There are going to be nay-sayers and people that doubt you, family included. Know this, people can't even see for others what they can't see for themselves. A lot of adults may not be able to understand your enthusiasm or charisma because many people are hardly ever happy in their workplace or are even passionate about what they do. With that being said you have to protect your peace. Don't allow negative people to halt the progress you make in any area of your life, believe in yourself even if everyone in the world is doubting you.

Positive people

-Sisters and brothers

-Best friend

-Next door neighbor

-Mom

Example

Negative People

-Grandma

-Co-worker in cubicle next to you

-Carmen (friend)

-Uncle Pat (on dad side)

Positive things/ habits

Negative things/ habits

-Praying everyday

-Watching tv

-Giving myself 1hr a day to do whatever I want (rest/ relax)

-Gossiping about negative things

-Drinking 8 cups of water daily

-Stress shopping or eating

-Reciting daily affirmations

-Not taking action towards your goals when you have free time to do so (procrastinating)

-Smiling or making sure you bring laughter and joy into your day

-Being selfish (not thinking of others)

Positive/ habits and people vs. Negative/ habits and people

●	●
●	●
●	●
●	●
●	●
●	●
●	●
●	●
●	●

●	●
●	●
●	●
●	●
●	●
●	●
●	●
●	●

●	●
●	●
●	●

FYI: Health

I felt it in my heart that I had to talk briefly about this important topic of health due to the health crisis in the world. I want all eyes reading this to know that your health matters so much more than your size. So please if you want to know more about taking care of your health look to health leaders such as Dr. Sebi and Queen Afua for further guidance. I can give you some basic tips that have helped me in my everyday life, like drinking 8-12 cups of water daily. Eating a great deal of fruits and vegetables I enjoy. Be super selective with your sugar intake for example I don't drink anything but water, give or take a homemade smoothie every now and then. I am vegan so the candy I prefer is dark chocolate and I enjoy eating my baked goods every once in a while. I don't want you to think I'm saying you have to do the same as myself, what I'm saying is that perhaps you can cut back from time to time on foods or snacks you know lack the proper nutrients your body needs to thrive.

Over the past few years, I have indulged in a variety of highly informative based documentaries that have helped me learn more about the state of agriculture, dietary choices, medication/ drugs and the food industries that effect our lives, and I suggest you do the same to stay informed with what is happening around us. We heavily rely on our bodies and its for that reason we intentionally need to make the choice to get up and move, allowing proper blood flow throughout our whole body. I'm not referring to the boring gym or Pilates routines that only work for a handful of people. Exercising should be fun so, I'm referring to dancing, yoga, bike riding, tennis or even kick boxing, I think it's important that you enjoy every moment of your life as much as possible and exercise should be a part of that no matter how you choose to burn those calories. I'm going to share something with you that you may or may not have heard before. You matter, your life is priceless, the world needs you and I need you for as long as humanly possible. So, take care of your health so you can be here to add value and joy in the lives of strangers and people you love most. The choices we make today turn into habits after 30 days which become a part of your lifestyle after 90 days. The younger you are creating these habits the better off you'll be. I want the tips I provided for you here to spare you from all disease, cancers, and premature death. Don't be reactive be proactive!

Chapter: 6
Next Chapter

Let me ask you a question, is your cup full? Are you the kind of person that can't be told anything because you already know everything? Is it hard having a conversation with you because your views are the only acceptable ones you believe could ever be true? I'm here to inform you that no one has or ever will know all that there is to know about everything in the universe. It would be wise to seek guidance whenever possible through mentorship. Outside of this book we all need guidance and support but it's not easy to find at times. I'm speaking from experience when I say this, and I want you to make sure whomever you choose for that experience is wise. That doesn't come with financial wealth at all times, while wanting a mentor who has reached the levels of success, we all desire is ideal, it's not always attainable. People who have experienced much in life have a wealth of knowledge they can share with you. Age shouldn't even be a factor when choosing a mentor, just trust your gut when your guided to someone. Our mindset shapes who we become, who we meet and can play a role with who we love and how we love. What you think about whether it's future success or your current circumstances, shapes your future, so watch what you feed your mind!

Values are important and I feel like they aren't talked about much so I thought this section would help bring interesting conversations back to the dinner table. Values are individual beliefs that motivate people to act in one way or another. Values are instilled in families when young and they stay with you until you move out and create a family of your own. Many families usually have similar values by which they were raised, but one thing I noticed is how those values aren't talked about in families. If you are unaware of your family's values, ask your (mom/ grandma/ aunt) or any female cousin, women usually are aware of this kind of thing. Both women and men should discuss vales at the dinner table with their children to enrich their souls with knowledge of who they are and why they do things the way they do them.

You have to prioritize what is of most importance to you in order to honor the value of time. Prioritizing is difficult but necessary to accomplish your goals. You can read Carol S. Dweck Ph.D. book "Mindset" to help reshape how you see where you are in life. Her book is very motivational, a feel-good read that will inspire positive change for your future. If you are someone who puts others first all the time despite your own needs, you are going to have to stop spreading yourself so thin. Right now, invest your time, money and energy into yourself so that in 5- 20 years you'll really be able to help the people you love and care for. A small sacrifice for a lifetime of reward, you just have to ask yourself if you think it'll be worth it, for you?

"For every reason it's not possible, there are hundreds of people who have faced the same circumstances and succeeded".

-Jack Canfield

Answer this, what do you choose going forward? This is your life and the choices you make can affect others, but they are yours to make. Once you've decided, you will be ready to execute. Most people on the path to change get stuck before they execute which leaves them unproductive as it pertains to their goals. Execution is key to success and Grant Cardone speaks on that in his book "10x Rule". His book goes over how putting forth the energy required to surpass your goal 10x ensures that you'll accomplish your goal and at times even surpass it. You have all the power needed to take ownership of your life and make the decisions required for your success.

*"Whether you think you can or think you can't,
you're right".*

-Henry Ford

Celebrities who got degrees	Celebrities who didn't go to college or dropped out
1. Natalie Portman	1. Halle Berry
2. Yara Shahidi	2. Liza Minnelli
3. Emma Watson	3. Matt Damon
4. Eva Longoria	4. Reese Witherspoon
5. John Legend	5. Julie Andrews
6. Lionel Richie	6. Jay Z
7. Lupita Nyong'o	7. Whoopi Goldberg
8. Cole Sprouse	8. Jessica Alba
9. Ken Jeong	9. Brad Pitt
10. Megan Markle	10. Ben Affleck
11. Mayim Bialik	11. Beyonce
12. Taraji P. Henson	12. Leonardo DiCaprio
13. Adam Sandler	13. Emma Stone
14. 2 Chains	14. Ryan Gosling
15. Wanda Sykes	15. Russell Simmons
16. Spike Lee	16. Anna Wintour
17. Bradley cooper	17. Rachel Ray
18. Sigourney Weaver	18. Keanu Reeves
19. Meryl Streep	19. Mark Wahlberg
20. Bridgit Mendler	20. Chris Rock
21. Jamie fox	21. Jill Scott
22. Shaquille O' Neal	22. Eddie Murphy

FYI The Earth's Survival

I already know what you're thinking, why such a heavy topic right? Well, I'm sure you know this, but we are dependent on the Earth's survival. When your home isn't clean it probably means you should pull out the brushes, broom, mop, bleach, rags, and pine sol. Today the Earth suffers because of our poor choices, whether it be global warming, the amount of plastic in the sea or the livelihood of animals going extinct. It's time to clean house and correct the mistakes our ancestors made so future generations don't have to suffer for our actions or inactions. You may think to yourself how I added to what has already resulted from years of wrongdoing before you were even born. Look, if we continue to point fingers we will get nowhere, truth is some of the people responsible are no longer with us, can you imagine what the world would look like if every generation thought that way? Every woman or man for her or him-self.

So here are some things we can all do to reverse the damage that has resulted:

1. Recycle as often as possible and encourage peers and family to do the same. Even if they don't grasp your suggestion, your influence will hopefully inspire change.

2. Go eco- friendly as often as possible so we can preserve mother nature. This includes eco-friendly cleaning supplies, using paper instead of plastic as often as possible and when using plastic remembering to recycle.

3. Cutting back from eating meat and dairy. As stated in Ed Winters book "This is Vegan Propaganda" The UN released a report

that spoke on how livestock is causing major problems that is negatively affecting our environment. The findings state that when dealing with problems of land degradation, climate change, air pollution, water shortage and water pollution and loss of biodiversity. Four years later, the UN then warned that a global shift towards a vegan diet was vital to save the world from hunger, fuel poverty, and the worst impacts of climate change.

This may feel like a lot to take in at once but try to digest this information in small sections so you can understand the severity of the information without getting overwhelmed. It's going to take all of us to see the change mother nature deserves, so we have to start and share to encourage others to do the same. The fate of Earth is in our hands, lets choose to do better and be better!

*Please Note: A vegan diet is mentioned in the above paragraph as a suggestion, do your own research to find out what diet works for your lifestyle. Whether it be paleo, carnivorous, pescatarian, keto, vegetarian or vegan.

Chapter: 7
Conclusion

You may face obstacles in life that challenge your values and when that happens you are often left with two choices, getting revenge or taking the high road. You know this is a challenge many adults face during different periods of their life. Revenge is nasty business and I say that based off the 7th law in "Universal Laws" the law of cause and effect. I know you can come up with 101 reasons why revenge would be a good idea so I'm not going to give energy to that. I'm going to share with you the reason why taking the high road is the way you should go vs. the latter. God doesn't miss a thing and if you believe that, you know all that anyone has coming to them will reach them, just a matter of time. Nature will handle it. You get to flex your, self-control muscle while staying focused on your goals and your growth. Remember not to give people the satisfaction of disturbing your peace, they can hold their breath waiting on it because you have bigger fish to fry. Attention goes where energy flows!

> *"Today's accomplishments were yesterday's impossibilities".*
>
> *Robert H. Schuller*

So, I ask you what is life? At your age right now how would you define it? If someone were to ask me that very question, I would say that life is a journey that can take us anywhere we want to go. I understand that everyone starts at different levels in life, financially, spiritually and mentally. You will be all set to achieve that of which you desire, as long as you focus and get your mind right. It can be easier for some and harder for others, to get where they want to go in life and that's okay, we have to just work with the hand we're dealt.

This is your life, no one can live it for you, act like you know this and move accordingly. Don't make the mistake of living your parent's life for them unless it's something you honestly choose for yourself. Parents understand as individuals our dreams and goals are different and it's almost always never too late to get started for yourself. Don't drag your child into the picture like they owe it to you to accomplish that of which you should have done, or still should do. Let your children live the life they choose and support them on their journey, life is meant to be enjoyed.

It's important for us to expect a lot from ourselves and to continually improve in our lives. Just like our parents expect a lot from us academically. Never allow your ambitious expectations to discourage you if you are not seeing progress as soon as you like. Some great things take time, I'm certain if you stay persistent and focused your goals will get achieved.

Times can get tough in life, I for one know all about that and I'm going to share a practice that can help anyone dealing with depression, anxiety, stress and illness. Meditation is a mindful practice that goes back to 1500 BCE and it's a practice done in many different ways by religious and spiritual people from all walks of life. There are three different types of meditation styles I'm going to share with you, the first being mantra based; where an individual would for example repeat a chant for strength, wealth or wellness. There are hundreds of chants available that are typically recited in the Hindu religion also known as "Sanatanadarma". The guided meditation is where many people start off because it's easier to follow and calming to the mind. Guided meditation can be found on YouTube, and you can even find it in the calm app which I highly recommend. The third way to meditate, I would call it a freestyle meditation because you can incorporate breathing techniques, semi-precious gemstones, candles, incense, burning sage and soft calming natural sounds, such as rain a spring meadow or waterfall. This third meditation style can be a little difficult if you try it without music or natural sounds, but I do dare you to try when your mind is ready. Thoughts will continuously be flowing and that's okay, it takes time to practice the art of quieting the mind. Prioritize this in your schedule even if it's just for 5 minutes at a time and this practice will help you have a peaceful state even in seemingly stressful situations. Mastering meditation like monks do in the Buddhist religion will help you see the world differently over time, allowing you total control over every aspect of self. I want that kind of freedom for you, but you have to want it for yourself.

Have you ever heard the saying gratitude will get you far in life? Well, it certainly is true especially when you think about "Universal Laws" (the "universal laws" can be found at the end of this chapter). Gratitude can come in many ways by verbal appreciation, financial gratuity for a service provided, a gift given, or favor offered. Sometimes gratitude can look like a wife keeping the house clean for her husband who likes a clean home after a long day of work. Kindness given will be kindness returned back to you according to the universal laws. I think we go through life expecting so much we forget that there are so many people who have much less than we do. I believe many people forget to share gratitude with God through prayer because we get so caught up in what we don't have or what we want. My mom told me the things we don't appreciate have a timer on them and they eventually disappear when we aren't grateful for what we have and don't take care of those people and items. Please stop reading for the next 2-3 minutes I want you to write down in the section provided on the following page all the people you are grateful for and on the other side of paper all the things you have that you are grateful for. I remember watching a really good interview with someone who spoke about how once many adults leave home, they barely make time to spend with their parents. Think about this, "majority of seniors make their transition, for men the average age is 73.5 and for women 79.3 years depending on how well they take care of themselves". Often times we all get busy in our own lives we forget to make time for those responsible for giving us life. You move out and sometimes leave the state or possibly the country and many people visit their parents twice a year. Multiply that by the sum of years they have to live based off the average life expectancy of seniors and you get the total amount of times you will probably spend with your parents. I am saying all this to give you an idea of how much real time you will have to spend with your loved ones before they pass on. Now I want you to think about that and possibly make some changes that will allow you to spend more time with the people you love. Make sure you take time to show people you appreciate them.

<u>Ex. Gratitude List</u>

- <u>**I am grateful for another day.**</u>

- <u>**I am grateful for my family.**</u>

- <u>**I am grateful for my income.**</u>

- <u>**I am grateful for the joy in my life.**</u>

- <u>**I am grateful for my home.**</u>

OR

- <u>**Thank you for my purpose!**</u>

- <u>**Thank you for my courage!**</u>

- <u>**Thank you for my strength!**</u>

- <u>**Thank you for today!**</u>

- <u>**Thank you for my support team!**</u>

GRATITUDE LIST

1.
2.
3.
4.
5.
6.
7.
8.
9.
10.
11.
12.
13.
14.
15.
16.
17.

Life is limitless and your life experiences are just that as well, being prepared for them is up to you. Don't be reactive like most people in the world, being proactive in life will save you time, energy, money and heart ache.

"Success is not final; failure is not fatal: it is the courage to continue that counts".

Winston S. Church hill

You are the author of your story, how it goes after it starts is up to you. You may have to reread this a few times as the occasional reminder to stay on track. Remember to never lose sight of what is important and make sure that once you create a goal you execute by taking the necessary steps required to accomplish it. If you don't succeed the first time, don't give up, understand with the right preparation your chances of failing go down drastically. That's why people create partnerships sometimes, to work with seasoned people in whichever field they choose to work in or create a business in because it can help you make fewer mistakes before launching. It's always good to seek help or advice when in question of anything, so don't be too chicken to ask for help when the time presents itself. This reading was the first step to positively changing your life and the next one is, well, you probably already guessed it "EXECUTION". You may very well not be ready but once you decide, it's go-time and once you start there's only one person that can get in your way, YOU! Don't let yourself down! Also, I won't wish you luck because you have determination so get busy and prove yourself right because I already knew you could do it. BELIEVE!

<u>12 Universal Laws</u>

1. Law of Divine Oneness:

The first and most foundational law of the universe is the law of divine oneness, which highlights the interconnectedness of all things. It says that beyond our senses, every thought, action and event is in some way connected to any and everything else.

2. Law of Vibration:

At a microscopic level, everything is in constant motion, vibrating at a specific frequency. This applies to matter but also one's personal frequency as well. This law says that our vibrational frequency can inform our lived experience.

3. Law of Correspondence:

This law states that patterns repeat throughout the universe, and on a personal level our reality is a mirror of what's happening inside us at that moment. Think "As above, so below. As within, so without."

4. Law of attraction:

Undoubtedly the most talked about universal law, the law of attraction is often used for manifestation. It says that like attracts like, and you get what you focus on. Not only that, but you have to believe what you're seeking is possible to obtain.

5. Law of Inspired Action:

Closely related to the law of attraction, the law of inspired action is all about taking those real, actionable steps to invite what we want into our lives. Often the inspiration comes from within. Inspired action is that gentle, internal nudge. "It's not always a plan of action."

6. Law of Perpetual Transmutation of Energy:

This law states that on an energetic level, everything in the universe is constantly evolving or fluctuating. Every action is preceded by a thought, with thoughts themselves having the power to eventually manifest in our physical reality.

7. Law of Cause and Effect:

Relatively straight forward, this law highlights the direct relation between actions and events. We can't see the effects right away, but they'll come back around.

8. Laws of Compensation:

The law of compensation relates closely to the law of attraction and the law of correspondence. "You reap what you sow" is the main take away, within the law stating your efforts will always come back to you positively If you are seeking something you must contribute in some way towards your goal.

9. Law of Relativity:

This law suggest that we are inclined to compare things in our world, but in reality, everything is neutral. Relativism exists in all things, and in the end, meaning comes down to our perspective and perception.

10. Law of Polarity:

This law says that everything in life has an opposite; good and evil, love and fear, warmth and cold. The key is understanding these are all two sides of the same coin.

11. Law of Rhythm:

Cycles are a natural part of the universe. Physically, you can think about the seasons on Earth. In our own lives, we can remember that integration is just as important as growth. We. Expect ourselves to be one way all the time, whether we are thinking about are health or even productivity, but it's not sustainable.

12. Law of Gender:

And lastly, the law of gender has to do with the masculine and feminine energy that exist in all things. Much of our society has historically operated from a masculine, "hustle and do "mentality, which doesn't allow for much room to just be.

These 12 laws are the most common laws that date back to ancient Kemetic times. I'm sharing them with you because as you go through life you will come across experiences that relate to the 12 laws stated. I encourage you to study them and go through life mindfully to avoid perhaps some of the side effects that occur from senseless mistakes.

Oh, Yea I Almost Forgot

If I'm being honest with you, I totally forgot about this important information I am getting ready to share with you on this page. But I know that it was meant for me to share because I didn't publish this book before remembering it! If you are inspired to start your own business/ company, the information that I am going to share with you is vital for your sanity. I found myself at 26 not even knowing most of this information even though I had a business at 9 years of age. When securing the perfect name for your business always do a google search, social media search and trademark search to know that your potential name isn't being used. If you run into even a similar variation, you may want to change your potential business name so that it stands out from any other existing company. Whether you're interested in an LLC or a trademark for your business just know if you don't make your business public and someone else has the same name as you, they automatically have the upper hand legally as it pertains to first exposure in the public.

Depending on your expertise you want to make sure that your name, logo and processes or inventions are protected at all times. By getting your LLC, necessary trademarks, copyrights and patents, you ensure that security. Do your research when it comes to all of this! Copyrights are usually seen in the writer space as well as in the music industry to name a couple. Copywrites protect your work from being plagiarized and used without compensation to the artist or creator.

Patents are extremely costly, but I would say worthy of the time and money put into them. They are the best way to ensure rights to a specific design, process, assembly or composition of matter. Patents can cost between $5,000- $20,000 each and though the process to secure your invention can be long once it's complete you'll always have ownership of it. You should always get your patents under your personal name, never under your business name because if you ever decided to sell your business, you would lose your rights to the patent. If you get the patent under your personal name, you will have the ability to make two sales. If the patent is required within whatever business, you are selling. Or you can have the ability to lease the patent to whomever you please creating passive income for yourself or your family. Patents make a great legacy, if you find yourself with an overflow of ideas you know will be beneficial to the future, I say patent it. Your family may be able to benefit from that small investment one day, whether they sell it, lease it or choose to take on the challenge of going forward with your idea once you are no longer here.

When you reach the levels of success most desired by many, people seek out financial advisers to help manage their funds and take care of their taxes. I came across some very troubling interviews with celebrities who were taken advantage of due to their trust in a licensed professional. What I learned is that you never let anyone else manage your money especially over the age of 18, whether it be a relative or licensed professional. Family can mismanage capital and financial advisers can steal and leave you in a bucket load of trouble with the IRS. So, I think it best to learn discipline when it comes to paying your bills and managing money overall so you can either oversee someone you higher to manage the business finances or handle the finances yourself. I highly recommend the dummies book series; they have plenty of books on a wide variety of topics that can help you navigate in whatever genre you need guidance in. May God bless on your journey to adulthood and in planning a successful future. Congratulations on getting this far, the rest is up to you!

About the Author

My name is Aneesa El Amin-Sims and this is just a bit about me. I was born and raised in Detroit, MI July 15, 1996 to my parents Delilah El Amin-Sims and Darryl Danub Sims. I am the fifth child out of six, three brothers and two sisters. I was home schooled until 5th grade when my sister and I were enrolled into a mix of public schools, one afro centric school and charter schools. My parents are far from perfect but they did open the window of our minds to the idea of being self- employed. While also sharing the importance of giving back and always being grateful for what we have, I will always be grateful to them for that. My inspiration for writing this book came from my own observation of the knowledge I had picked up from reading books, listening to podcast/ interviews and learning through my own trials and tribulations. I pray that you find this book beneficial to your life. May peace be with you always.

<u>GLOSSARY</u>

Ambitious- greatly desirous; eager, requiring or showing much effort.

Assets- is a resource with economic value that an individual, corporation, or country owns or controls with the expectation that it will provide a future benefit.

Bankruptcy- is a legal proceeding carried out to free individuals or businesses from their debts.

Bullying- abuse and mistreatment of someone vulnerable, an aggressive behavior in which someone intentionally and repeatedly causes another person injury or discomfort.

Charisma- a special power that some people have naturally that makes them able to influence other people and attract their attention and admiration.

Copy right- the legal right granted to an author, composer, playwright, publisher, or distributor to exclusive publication, production, sale, or distribution of a literary, musical or artistic work.

Credit card- a credit card is a financial tool offered by a bank as a type of loan, with a line of revolving credit that you can access with your card account.

Determination-the process of controlling, influencing, or deciding something.

Enthusiasm- great excitement for or interest in a subject or cause.

Frazzled- in a state of extreme physical or nervous fatigue and agitation.

Humility- is an attitude of spiritual modesty that comes from understanding our place in the larger order of things.

Investment- is an asset or item acquired with the goal of generating oncome or appreciation.

Judgement- the ability to judge, make a decision, or form an opinion objectively, authoritatively, and wisely, especially in matters affecting action; good sense; discretion.

Land degradation- the decline in the overall quality of soil, water or vegetation condition commonly caused by human activities.

Latter- near or towards the end of something.

Leveraging- investing with borrowed money as a way to amplify potential gains.

Liability- something for which one is liable; an obligation, responsibility, or debt.

LLC- a limited liability company (LLC) is a business structure in the U.S. that protects its owners from personal responsibility for its debts or liabilities.

Mantra- a sacred verbal formula repeated in prayer, meditation, or incantation, such as an invocation of a God, a magic spell, or a syllable or portion of scripture containing mystical potentialities.

Mindful- attentive, aware, careful.

Patent- is an exclusive right granted for an invention, which is a product or a process that provides, in general, a new way of doing something, or offers a new technical solution to a problem.

Perspectives- a mental view or outlook.

Plagiarized-to steal and pass off as one's own.

Proactive- acting in advance to deal with an expected difficulty; anticipatory.

Rat race- an exhausted routine that leaves no time for relaxation.

Reactive- tending to be responsive or to react to a stimulus.

Surpass- to become better, greater, or stronger than, to go beyond

Trademark- a name, symbol, or other device used to identify and promote a product or service, especially an officially registered name or symbol that is thereby protected against use by others.

Values- principles that help you decide what is right and wrong and how to act in various situations.

Wholistic- represents the entirety of something.

REFRENCES

Harvard business review by: Jeffrey J. Selingo May 31, 2016
http://hbr.org/2016/05/two-thirds-of-college-grads-struggle-to-launch-their-careers

http://www.successcds.net/learn-english/essays-suicide-among-students-due-to-parental-pressure

http://www.uscourts.gov/news/2021/05/03/new-bankruptcy-filings-plummet-381-percent

ED Winters "This is Vegan Propaganda"

http://www.mindbodygreen.com/articles/the-12-universal-laws-and-how-to-practice-them

BOOK REFRENCES

1. Contract Law for dummies by: Scott J. Burnham

2. Grit by: Angela Duckworth

3. Rich dad Poor dad by: Robert T. Kiyosaki

4. Mindset by: Carol S Dweck Ph.D.

5. 10x Rule by: Grant Cardone

6. The Art of War by: Sun Tzu

7. 5 Second Rule by: Mel Robbins

8. How to Talk to Anyone by: Leil Lowndes

9. Extreme Ownership by: Jocko Willink & Leif Babin

10. 48 Laws of Power by: Robert Greene

11. This is Vegan Propaganda by: ED Winters

12. The Secret Principals of Genius by: I. C. Robledo

13. Intellectual Foreplay: Eve Eschner Hogan and Steven Hogan

My prayer for you dear reader is that you heal from any trauma you may have experienced in your life. I pray that God helps you find self-love in your life and that you discover all the gifts God has blessed you with. You are a blessing whether you know it or not and I pray that you are blessed profusely and that your life is a beautiful journey of your choosing. Remember freedom is enjoying every moment of your life without feeling limited by a job, business, other people or yourself! Peace be with you always!

9 798218 224349